# DRAGGING THE LAKE

## BOOKS BY ROBERT THOMAS

*Door to Door*
*Dragging the Lake*

# DRAGGING THE LAKE

POEMS BY

## ROBERT THOMAS

*Yes I thought I spied my old time used to be*
*And it was not nothing, honey, but a cypress tree*

— Leadbelly, "Roberta"

*And what there is between a man and a woman.*
*And in which darkness it can best be proved.*

— Eavan Boland, "Quarantine"

CARNEGIE MELLON UNIVERSITY PRESS
PITTSBURGH 2006

## ACKNOWLEDGMENTS

I am grateful to the editors of the following publications, in which some of the poems in this book first appeared, sometimes in other forms: *Artful Dodge, The Atlanta Review, The Capilano Review, CutBank, The Iowa Review, The Marlboro Review, New England Review, Nimrod International Journal, Rattle, Slate,* and *The Threepenny Review.* "Dragging the Lake" was awarded second prize in the *Nimrod/* Hardman Awards Pablo Neruda Prize competition. I also want to thank the National Endowment for the Arts for a grant that gave me precious time to complete this book.

Cover photo: Josef Koudelka, *France. 1974. Region of Provence-Alpes-Côte d'Azur. The Bouches-du-Rhône 'department'. Town of Saintes-Maries de la Mer.*

Book design: Allison Pottern

The publication of this book is supported by a grant from the Pennsylvania Council on the Arts.

Library of Congress Control Number 2005926191
ISBN-13: 978-0-88748-450-6
ISBN-10: 0-88748-450-6

PENNSYLVANIA
COUNCIL
ON THE

ARTS

10  9  8  7  6  5  4  3  2  1

# Engulfed Cathedral

The Varieties of Love 9

The Muse's Complaint: Take This Job and Shove It 11

Four Parallel Lines 12

Sleepwalker 14

Dragging the Lake 15

# Dancing the Szatmari

The Invention of Silk 25

Fast Angel 27

Night Shift 28

Song of the Soft-Shoe Sirens 30

Diary of One Who Vanished 31

# Tuning Pegs

Galileo's Notes 53

Aurora 54

The Origin of Poetry 62

Still Life with Pears 63

Concerto in E Minor 65

*The tiny grapes*
*Glazed themselves so softly in the soft tuft*
*Of butterflies, it was hard to name*
*Which vine, which insect, which wing,*
*Which of you, which of me.*

—James Wright

# Engulfed Cathedral

# THE VARIETIES OF LOVE

**1**

Jan and her boyfriend rented movies,
stayed up all night, and made love after each film.
This, to Jan, was sublime: sex with the afterimage
of a blue car driving past orange shop windows,
mannequins illuminated by headlights
through the slow back-and-forth of wipers.
Two hours later, the black-and-white grain
of concrete panned by searchlights
as a man struggles over the Berlin Wall.
Near morning, a handful of skaters crisscross a lake
on the outskirts of a mining town, no soundtrack
but the *thresh* of blades on ice.

**2**

There are four kinds of lovers: those who love
the roses—Ehigala, Mojave, Satchmo, Lemon Pillar,
Whisky Mac—those who love their parts—auricle,
corymb, panicle, rhachis, umbel—those who love
the mulch—pine bark, cedar chip, cocoa hull, leaf mold,
potash—and those who love the cities they come from—
Lijiang, Tashkent, Nootka, Algeciras, Baton Rouge.

**3**

Patrick died in his bed in his pajamas,
his son brushing strands of white hair
from his forehead, his wife on his right
holding his hand, his mistress on his left
holding the other, his eyes staring
at the ceiling, a Prime Minister
enjoying the brief unity
his Parliament grants him,
now that the war has begun.

**4**

The art studio was near the ocean, across from the zoo:
at night Alison could hear the lions and the surf.
Once she got in through a back gate after closing

and watched the flamingoes sleep, black beaks
curved into their breasts,
and realized she couldn't love Beth anymore.
It was because of the edge, the scent, the watershed:
the carved, the damp, the effulgent—
everything that was part of her now.

5

The gold of the silk-screened snow
on the card still on Tina's dresser, the gold of the sun
that rose as she ground her coffee, the gold
that burst from the barrel as she pushed
the trigger with both thumbs, the gold threads
of the blanket they found her curled on,
knees tucked up so she would fit
within the green, symmetrical borders.

6

Whenever Enrique was in New York,
he went to see the painting of the almond tree.
If he had to choose between the painting's destruction
and the death of his own family, of course
the choice would be clear. But what if he had to choose
between the painting and the life of the man
who read his meter through a rusted grate,
or the lives of some chophouse diners
in a distant city? Could he still be sure?
The charged blue of the sky—how it picked up
the branches' undertones—that was irreplaceable.

7

What surprised Nathaniel was not that there was no God,
nor that he had stopped believing in one,
but that his belief had ceased without his noticing.
How many shades of green there were
in the wilderness, how many evenings in each throat,
how naked the salt lick stood in the city square.

## THE MUSE'S COMPLAINT:
### TAKE THIS JOB AND SHOVE IT

You watched as I rode my bike for a butter stick,
watched from the choir as I returned to my pew
from the communion rail, counting the red tiles.
When I ran out of gas next to a garlic farm
and went down a furrow to the dark garage,
when I danced at my brother's wedding
stomping my boots without wasting one drop
of champagne, you were there. You loomed,
likening me to a diamond can opener
or a one-woman bevy of quail, but always
likening me. I bled and to you I was a page-turner,
wept and for you the mokihana bloomed red
on Mt. Waialeale. You don't even know
that Johnny PayCheck died last month,
whose obituary said he shot a man in an Ohio
watering hole, capitalized the "C" in his name
a few years later, and wrote three great songs,
one of which is remembered. What about your
obit? That you fed lambs with an eyedropper?
Milked the Great Bear? I've had it up to here
with your marching band: I'm taking off
my spandex epaulettes. The next time I toss
my flaming baton, I'll be in another state
when it comes down. On your honeymoon
I'll be the aa, the glorious, trillion-spined
black lava slicing through your flip-flops.

# Four Parallel Lines

## Rose Window

I could live alone in a studio, practicing Debussy's *Engulfed Cathedral* on the piano after my morning walk to the bakery. The sound of those bells is nothing like the Byzantine chimes of the Greek Orthodox Church down the street. Those people scare me with their love of eggs! I have seen them solemnly carry loaves of Easter bread into the vestibule and never emerge. The sound is not like the clang of the streetcar cord the passenger yanks to get out. It is a sound you hear only in those impossible chords, or perhaps if you live in the Paris catacombs and listen to the light of a rose window as it resounds through ten feet of stone.

## Pop and Hiss

I could have died years ago, and now my wife would be married to a master chef who can debone a chicken while leaving the flesh intact. They would have a cactus garden full of cholla, and one saguaro. They would have repainted the house the same color, but their Christmas tree would be larger than ours, almost piercing the ceiling, with a thousand white bulbs flashing in the living room next to the cabinet, which would contain different CDs, Madonna and Sting. They would have to shout to be heard over the hiss and pop of bacon on the griddle (just enough to add a bit of flavor), and it would only deepen their love.

## The First Mirror

I could live in the desert, moving from water to water. For a man to look into his own eyes for the first time—the creation of fire was nothing to that. To lower his face to the surface and drink of the sun and the date palm—surely in the desert one would think of that—the silver, feathery leaves. The disturbance as a coin, or a handful of seeds, was dropped into the pool. Not knowing what would emerge, whether it would come from above or below. At noon he watched a woman stretch to break off a palm to fan herself, and knew he wanted her for his wife, but it was when he saw her image in the water cleaving the branch from the tree that he first knew love.

## TAKING NOTE

I could be an owl on the roof of a barn. The dark landscape would be a rippling jewel with a thousand facets, and I would monitor each one with the power of consciousness unhindered by self-consciousness. It would be as if you could hear the conversation of children under the Ferris wheel lights across the city, how two of them plot to grab the barrette from the sleek hair of the third and hide it in a drainpipe, or you could see the couple across the plaza through a gap in their blinds as he takes off his watch, laying it carefully next to the lamp like a sacred vestment, she cocks her head to one side, then the other, removing her earrings, and you see that both of them are too gentle and ruthless to say a word. No one ever said that God weeps when a sparrow falls, only that He takes note.

## SLEEPWALKER

One night I found you pumping
from the neighbors' well. Drinking
like a dog: nothing as fresh as the tang
of iron. I let you finish, watching your thirst
unsheathe. When I woke you, a shudder
like the shadow of a frenulum,
the narrow band that keeps a moth's wings
from tearing apart in flight, crossed your face
before you recognized me, or was it
just after, the moment just after
I spoke your name, when you remembered
it was yours.

In the morning you have bruises,
inky thumbprints on your hips
from bumping the porch grill, but you've never
truly hurt yourself, and I never know
whether to wake you, you seem so serene,
as if walking on water and all the ocean
were yours—not just the kelp
and herring that glint in the sun,
but the deeper layers, eels and rays
in the vertical dusk, even the blind crustaceans
in absolute dark, where light has nothing
to do with what makes you thrive.

And then I witness the awful moment
when the part usurps the whole,
and the vast, porous surface of what you see with
shrinks to the chink of an eye.

## DRAGGING THE LAKE

**I**

When Desdemona says her night prayers
in Verdi's opera and her voice
suddenly descends an octave into the blue and bronze
waters of Venice and it's clear
that of course she would have driven Othello mad,
I think of you singing that Elvis Costello
hit about dragging the lake,
your voice faltering, finding itself and
faltering again, the arch of your throat
an architectural treasure, a Bridge of Sighs
down which the condemned walk without looking back.

**II**

At Half Moon Bay you buy a sack of salt
water taffy as if a purse of loose pearls,
as if you could make our suburban home
reek of the ocean, lock its baroque aroma
in the functional cabinets of our pantry.

**III**

As you show me what to do
with my lips, I think of Bridget,
patron of blacksmiths and poets,
who taught men how to whistle.
Milk snakes emerge from their holes
on her February feast. Oystercatchers
pierce the sky with their long orange bills.
Pagan goddess, Christian saint, she greeted
a visiting priest by turning her bath water into beer.

## IV

The cherry tree bursts
with white like a flashbulb.
Photographers once risked their hands
and eyes, igniting vials of magnesium powder,
so powerful is the love of the image.
Your sleeves catch fire in the blooms.

## V

Remember when I cut my hair and hitched
that ride on a truck full of artichokes and
the farmer kept telling me he didn't expect
his employees to work as hard as he did, just
half as hard, and he was drinking red wine
from a paper cup when I got off at the 95
junction and walked past the warehouses
and auto shops and rang your doorbell—
one of those antique mechanical chimes—
at four A.M. and your pregnant roommate
put on her cutoffs and opened the door?
You woke for an instant and then returned
to a white ox wandering in scrap auto parts,
pausing to drink from the shell of a headlight.

## VI

Even chess grandmasters must get bored,
must long for a provocative game
more than a victory. One day we made
our bed, and found a single gold stud,
the provenance of which we both claimed—
truthfully, I believe—to be unaware.

**VII**
Susanna's aria in Mozart's *Marriage*:
each note sharp as a pin
thrust into a voodoo doll.
Does she want to kill Figaro,
compel him to love her, or both?
Her hands move too fast for the eye:
*Come la man mi pizzica,* she sings:
how my hand tingles!

**VIII**
How could I not love someone
whose quest is for just the right place to read
every book in the library? *The Last Goodbye*
on a seedy boat moored in the Sacramento delta,
your ankles dangling at dusk in the dirty river.
A bare white hotel room in Paris
with one white rose on the edge
of the porcelain sink: Colette's *Vagabond.*
Poetry on a yellow bench in Cuernavaca,
next to a child who asks you questions
in a language you can't understand,
a blue lizard on the back of his hand
as still as a tattoo, and as indelible.

## IX

What is our plea, guilty or not guilty? In one year in the U.S.A.,
153,310 from lung cancer, the population of Salinas, where my
mother went to the coroner's office to identify the body of her
sister, found at home slumped over a chenille chair.

Guilty or not guilty? 85 from rheumatic fever, the number of dark red
petals—almost black—on one bloom of an Othello rose, and 831
from the accidental discharge of firearms, the number of colors
recognizable by the human eye.

6,189 from uterine cancer, the number of paintings in the Louvre,
where the angel in the *Virgin of the Rocks* looks out at the viewer
with that mixture of incredible tenderness and the skepticism of a
citizen of Milan.

16,516 from AIDS, the height in feet of Mount Ararat, where Noah's
ark came to rest with its cargo of geese and gibbons.

19,491 by murder, 30,535 by suicide, together the population of our
hometown, South San Francisco, purchased in 1890 by G.F. Swift
for his stockyards and named after South Chicago.

206,212 from acute myocardial infarction, the population of Madison,
where my mother became an anesthesiologist to learn how to
end pain without ending life.

535,575 from all cancers, the population of Portland, where my father
left two wives to move to Oakland, and my mother, the third, fell
in love with a surgeon's hands.

Guilty or not guilty? We who know that all it takes to shipwreck a life
is a paper boat quietly lacerating a pond without troubling the
swans.

**X**

If you are dying and imagine yourself rising
above the television, the parades and police barricades
on the news, rising above the armoire
with its regiment of black socks,
and looking down on your body in gray pajamas
and shearling slippers, tell me: in what way
is that different from rising for real?
It's not that unusual to meet someone who knows you better
than you know yourself, so isn't imagination sometimes
more accurate than experience? The glass of water,
the book of Hemingway with the blue
hard cover and silver lettering on the spine,
wire hangers strewn like lilies on the foot of the bed.
Through the smudged window the unmarked slab
of the driveway, a car parked at an angle
as if in a hurry, but there is no hurry.
The chatter of sparrows,
annoying as answering machines.
The forgiveness the dead extend to the living:
passionate and absolute.

## XI

Today I'm so in love I could write an ode
to all the women who've rejected me:
Beth, who with such glee regaled me
with the story of her fisherboy affair,
what the lobster pots and shrimp nets
sprawled on his shack floor did to her,
and then told me about the florist's son
who knew just how to trim the stems
of peonies; Alison, who let me feed her
French fries and candied apple at the fair
and knew more than anyone about Flaubert,
how his sublime green beetle was translated
obscenely as a butterfly by some hack;
Lois, who told the whole class how she rode
her bike from the Back Burner Blues Band
and found two snakes copulating in the vines
across her front porch—it was her utterly
natural pronunciation of the word, *copulating*,
that made clear in her case I wouldn't even try;
and Alexandra, who stood at the back of the jazz
festival and would have given every strand of her
red kinky hair to burnish Ron Carter's double bass
as he thoughtfully undressed *Stella by Starlight* . . .

## XII (DUET FOR BRUSHES AND BASS)

Night and day
Jade visions (take 2)
Too much sugar for a dime
Just one of those things
Detour ahead
Don't forget to mess around
Too marvelous for words
But not for me

If you could see me now
Well, you needn't
Umbrella man
Finger buster
Smooth operator
Body and soul
Experience unnecessary
Don't mean a thing

What is there to say?
I know that you know
Alright, okay, you win
How important can it be?
Enter, evening (soft line structure)
If I knew then (what I know now)
You're not the kind
It never entered my mind

**XIII**

Toward a backwater of the Feather River,
ten miles from Paradise, California,
we walk the dry aisles of a walnut grove
eating bacon and mayo, thinking of the kid
at the deli who'd sent us here for a picnic
after telling us about Brenda Hurley,
a beautician, as fast and beautiful herself
as the teal blue Jaguar XK that stopped
once for gas in Paradise, how he'd never
forget the blurry screech of Neil Young's
guitar from its ten speakers as he filled the tank.

Brenda and Phil left choir practice one evening,
and even though the clouds were low as the church
basement ceiling, they came here, Brenda said later,
talking about nothing, whether to bring a salad
to Sunday dinner at her mom's, and she lifted
the .22 from her purse as calmly as if it were
a cigarette case, sterling and monogrammed,
and shot Phil Hurley in the heart, "the nicest
guy in the world," everyone still says, and she's
never denied it. And you—who would cut off
your own hand before you'd part a spider
from its web—you stand with me at the edge
and fling crusts with the small, perfect
muscles of your wrist to shining blue ducks
in praise of Brenda's unforgivable nerve
and dazzling black hair, and the crumbs
float like medals from a forgotten war
that forged the perilous borders of our world.

# DANCING THE SZATMARI

## THE INVENTION OF SILK

What begins with bone
buttons and nylon straps
ends with two people ice fishing
on Lake Darling in North Dakota,
seeking pike in underwater kelp beds,
their lures glowing green in blue ice.

Salt on the wrist ends with a conversation
next to a flashing neon lime:
*Do you want the last one? Don't forget
your portfolio. I said I'd be there and
I'll be there. Next to the water fountain
with the sparkplug spigot.*

What begins on a Macy's escalator
ends with a passion forever defined
by the smell of fennel charred in olive oil:
the pattern—the ache—of two people
when one wants to become human
and the other for just one oh sweet
fucking Christ one instant finned
or hooved or invertebrate.

An evening of champagne and peaches
ends with parings of talk
left on the table. *Don't tell me
what I already know. You think
you're the March of Dimes.* I never
said that. *The Doge of Venice
with your waterfront view and pink
marble façade. You thought it. You thought
of everything: that the lions are weeping,*

*noble and prescient.* Noble, one of those words
I predict is about to come back
into fashion, as in She's a noble bitch.

Let's call it a day. *No, let's call it*
*the time it takes the sulky earth to rotate*
*once on its axis.* Don't talk about silk:
the silkworm must have been thinking
of some noble bitch like you
when he got his big idea.

## FAST ANGEL

You slip into the back seat of the old Packard.
The young man behind the wheel (Jim, I hear you say)
starts the motor and turns onto the wet macadam.
It's just the two of you now. He stares head-on
at the quarter moon, knowing he's got it worried,
gunning the car till it skips, a flat rock
over the blacktop, making that eerie blue whine,
a fast angel coming in on one holy wing.
He doesn't have to look in the mirror
to know what you're doing back there.
Something, not light, shines on your neck and instep.
Even in the scalloped leather upholstery
your body starts to recognize a pattern, a curling
resonance with its own secret form, and soon
it seizes on it everywhere: the smell of sorrel trees—
squeezed from sour leaves by the relentless
rain like hard cider from an iron press—
that hits when you jack open the window;
and the rough sheen of the air itself,
chafing your skin like a flimsy rag of raw silk.
Now when you look out the back window
all you see is a blur of red ricochet
off the perfect black facets of the storm
and get redder as it recedes
toward where you left me standing on the slick
crush of mica. I still feel the finish
of the chrome handle, hear the *shunk* of the door.
There is nothing between you and the whetted horizon.

## NIGHT SHIFT

From the hospital roof,
where even in winter I take my break,
I can see the lights of a night game
at the high school, and know my family is asleep
in the crosshatched shadows beyond the diamond.

Rick takes good care of the kids,
that's a fact. I'm in charge of the mainframe;
I keep the mag drums humming
till the day shift comes. There's not much
to the job: the machine's obsolete
as a steamboat, enduring as a Philco.
The hospital won't upgrade, and the scientists
don't care. Even what we call them—
not genetic engineers or enzymologists
but "scientists"—marks them
for extinction, as if they were blacksmiths
or bootleggers adding peaches to a tub of corn mash.

Rick doesn't drink a lot, but I know
he likes to pour one to keep him company with the remote
after I've left for work. It's the *idea* of it
that attracts him, but then so much of what attracts us
to anything is the idea, isn't it? Like me
and that Brad Pitt resident—what *was* that?
The idea that someone who's had no sleep
for forty-eight hours is exciting, edgy?
The idea of his clean hands
on the unit's thermostat, turning up
the fan? The idea that I'd find myself
if only I could be kissed
all the way to the third vertebra
in the same durable khaki slacks
I wear to crunch data? Well,
there are worse ideas, not that I'd ever
cheat on Rick. No matter
how good it was with some man in a mask
and blue scrubs, I'd be thinking of him:

how he hates feeding Hotwire,
as if any bull terrier worthy of the name
should hunt down her dinner,
and how he's too proud to read a bedtime story,
insists on making one up, some stopgap tale—
even Emma laughs at him—the fox
who forgot his phone number, the black cloud
who learned to tell time. I do love him,
whatever that means. I think it means
I know he's lost, too,
and that it feels good to say God bless him,
damn this dogwatch and have mercy on us
now and at the hour of the EKG,
because I believe prayer is *make believe,*
and because of a faint gingery smell in the air
of snow that will not fall, not tonight.

## SONG OF THE SOFT-SHOE SIRENS

Yes, go to your muses
if that's what you want. God rigged the gig
from the start, and we lost the singing prize
to those grisettes. They've got the edge
when it comes to equipment: a crystal pickup
and a boombox to die for. They've got all
the edges down. We can't believe they told you
our tongues shriek in short hooked beaks.
Cut the engines and listen. What we sing
is this. Decide for yourself. Then tell us
that you can tell our song from the one
your mother sang to your amazed father
before you were born, before he strapped on
his iron regalia and left for the trenches
and she put on her glasses to go back to her books,
their durable green spines already open on her desk.

## DIARY OF ONE WHO VANISHED

> *". . . in a telephone receiver, in the dust of centuries-old registers, in the flag
> that flapped above the Castle in a mad whirl: yes, everywhere music . . ."*
> — Leoš Janáček

Brno, 25 April 1927, at night

My dear Kamila,

It terrifies me: the flowers are alive.
Dwarf iris insinuated itself against
my ankles this morning as I walked

to market for your strawberries. *Your.*
I'm a cad. I'd wolfed them by the time
I got home and, anyway, you've kept

yourself far enough that in this land
where roads are only half rests between
ruts, you might as well be in Budapest

dancing the szatmari with some hussar.
Yes, I'm terrified, and jealous and tired.
Zdenka was in one of her moods again,

banging cabinets while I tried to work,
pink hand-painted handles shivering
in her aftershock. The orchestration

of wood and rattling china was so
distinct I rushed to note it down:
I'll make it timpani and glockenspiel

and get my revenge. And your David
is well, I trust? Off to Prague or even
Vienna, I suppose, looking for a deal:

---

Note: *In 1919 Janáček completed his song cycle* Diary of One Who Vanished, *the text a set of
poems by Josef Kalda ("beautiful verses about gypsy love," in Janáček's words). During the last 10
years of his life Janáček wrote over 700 love letters to Kamila Stösslová, over 300 during the last
16 months alone.*

a commode from the reign of one
of the Louies, a dog tapestry. Ha! How
can we live like this? It can't go on,

as we've said for ten years, my gypsy,
my foie gras, spread on a bed of good
black bread, your black hair spilling

over the edge like Astrakhan caviar.


Brno, 26 April 1927

Dearest Kamila,

I was able to work today! Zdenka was acting
as if nothing was on her mind but apricots
she plucked to dunk in jars of salted juice,

and she bit her tongue while I stroked
that damn note over and over. You have to
do that sometimes to get it to come round.

First you tickle the key as if it were dusted
with a gloss of talc, then palpate the groove
until you find its pulse, and then you pound

until your knuckles bleed. *Then* you know
if you're anywhere near the map's X that
marks the treasure, *if* angle Y from poplar

to spire to the sunset's horizon point
on the vernal equinox hasn't changed
since the mapmaker scrawled his chart.

What a business I'm in, Kamila, not like
your slick husband, the Merry Merchant
of Prague, selling silks for a profit almost

as handsome as he is. You don't need
to tell me. I know: if you prick his dumb
thumb, my rose, blood flows; I know he

hath eyes, and sees the same white neck
I see under your red fox fur. I can't stop
thinking of it. I know I'm not being fair.

We're not so different, David and I. It can't
be easy to go down one more flea market's
back streets hoping it will be the one where

boulevards of bric-a-brac conceal something
real. Maybe it's not so different from writing
another aria, and there's no reason for you

to leave him, none at all. At least not today,
when the lilac, a spraying queen in heat,
shares its perfume with the whole garden.


Brno, 3 May 1927

My Kamilka,

The finches woke me up early, clicking
like maniacs. I'm serious: that rhythm
of a ratchet wheel just like the chit-chat

I heard at the asylum: *What's my name?*
Jesus Came. *Where's my home?* Cage
of Rome. *What is love?* Squirt and shove.

I transcribed it faithfully, spent two weeks
in the women's ward to get the inflections
just right for Míla's mother in my *Destiny*.

I don't know why I ever thought I had to
leave home. My first memory is Mother
scaring me in our apiary: bees hidden

in darkness, I saw only the glistening
of honey, no buzz but the quiet hum
of wing muscles warming a winter hive.

Have you seen the cave paintings of men
with torches terrorizing a hive with fire
so they can gorge on its honey? What a

species we are, Kamila! Mother explained
how drones first have to get used to a new
queen's scent or else they'll kill her, and so

you plug the hole between her and the hive
with a cork of candied sugar thick enough
that by the time they eat through to her

they know her smell enough to let her live.
It's easy to botch. Red finches, you know,
sing their silky lays only at rest in the elms.

When they fly, it's that raucous ack-ack.
That's the sound I want! *Can't get back?*
Chop and hack. *How to lick?* Hush-hush,

quick. *Who there knocks?* Roots, rags, rocks.
That's the tune for my *House of the Dead!*
No harp or violin but three saws and a file's

harsh rasp, scraping at the prisoners' chains.


Brno, 11 May 1927

Kamila, my Kamila,

I can hear Zdenka dusting the piano:
the woman has no more feel for music
than the cat when she spots a goblin

under the buffet and bounds down
from the keyboard to corner it. Now
you'll be angry, say I'm unfair to her:

maybe so. It's fifty years since I opened
my studio door to a fourteen-year-old.
She had talent—all right, *has* talent.

Her fingers found as many overtones
in the keys as her lovesick taskmaster
in her eyes: tense, sardonic, tender.

Was it wrong? The questions we ask!
To say she was a child would have been
lying to a child, and soon I loved more

than long fingers and short bangs—I swear
sometimes she looked like a pretty Emperor
Napoleon with that baby-fat, willful gaze—

and then I loved everything she touched,
from the silver saltcellar in which she dipped
the cucumber slices I offered her, to the bowl

of daffodils she brashly rearranged on my desk,
destroying me. That's when she became a need,
when through her I could love even my father's

clock on the mantel as it promised her arrival.
When she said she'd marry me, how could I
have foreseen the day I'd need someone else,

someone who could teach me to love something
else, or was it only to love the same things again,
the table strewn with blotched pages, blue chairs,

the smell of untouched, coffee-soaked cake
still on last night's plate, and the white sill
my inkwell rests on as I write you this letter?

Hukvaldy, 8 June 1927

You, my dark dove,

I'm treating myself to a shot of slivovitz, just
a sliver. All one needs is good Czech brandy,
an inconspicuous drink but strong *inside*,

a storm in my throat. I'm celebrating, I'm
dancing a *dumka*. And do you know why?
One syllable in your letter, that *Tvá* you tossed

off like a diva dropping a ducat for her servant
to pluck from a gutter. *Yours*: I've been waiting
to hear it for ten years. Why can't our spouses

see how innocent we are! I swear your breasts
are smooth as the piano's ivory after our Maria
has polished it with schnapps. I've come so far!

Or is it not so far at all? I learned to play Bach
on keys Mother chalked on our kitchen table.
In a village like this, for my father to be cantor

was almost enough to make us nobility, only
without the frill of money. It's hard to believe
we were still slaves to those Hapsburg fops,

Franz and Sisi. Rulers? Viennese pastries!
You call me unjust. The Empress *was* great:
she not only wrote sonnets but built a gym

in the winter palace for her calisthenics.
Generous, bold—how can I blame them
for not seeing beyond empire, its hierarchy

as baroque as an apple and elderberry strudel.
Why *would* they think the world would listen
to Moravian ditties as it did to Mozart's wigs?

Not even my father would have dared imagine.
I never told you, but I thought I saw him once,
sipping coffee, reading the news at the back

of the Prague café where you and I nibbled
on Linzer torte. I didn't interrupt him, nor
did he disturb us, yet that was the moment

I knew I had his blessing. He blessed *us*,
the crumbs on our lips, our furtive hands.
I know he didn't love me when I was born,

so why, suddenly, now? This ordinary man
in a brown vest in a grubby, remote corner
of the Empire, looking like an ancient king

in exile with no desire to return to his home,
adding a half teaspoon of sugar to his coffee,
riffling pages with ink-stained fingers, stirring.


                Hukvaldy, 10 June 1927

Dear Soul,

Zdenka teases me about our "estate,"
but I love this cottage. I know I've
made mistakes too large for anyone

to forgive. Marrying Zdenka was one,
and divorcing her worse. Marrying her
a second time was like the Archduke

riding his open car through Sarajevo.
I do thank the War for three blessings.
First, with all the soldiers at the front,

my chorus was full of girls: I heard
for the first time the female voice's
nonhuman range. Men always sing

*about* something with their voices
of thunder. Women are lightning,
blue shock transfixing a waterfall.

Second, of course, we were liberated.
Not only Prague freed to be Prague,
but Vienna to be Vienna! An empire

freed of itself. No longer was a man
asked to be a stout hero, only a man
drinking a smoke beer in Letna Park

at a table of cast iron under the lilacs.
Never in history had so much blood
been shed for the freedom to flirt and

to daydream in one's own language.
Third, in 1917 I saw you in Luhačovice
for the first time, twirling your parasol

as you left a patisserie. You always
had something—an apricot kolache,
a branch of pear blossoms plucked

on a whim from a stranger's garden—
to beckon me with a casual distraction
that burned then, on that brisk Friday

morning, and still does, on this one.


Frankfurt, 30 June 1927, late

Kamilka, my darling,

I'm exhausted but can't bear to wait
till morning to tell you: the concert
was a conquest. There was none of

that German pomp and pompadour:
we don't need *that* anymore. Ilona
skated on the keys, light as a dragonfly

on the Danube, but when she was wild,
she was the river itself, a white dragon.
I got your letter, but why thank me?

I could never forget how your sweet
husband gave Zdenka and me bacon
and milk during the War. To be able

now to repay him (with the interest
I know he appreciates!) so you can
keep coal in your grate now that he

is no longer in a position to and—
now that I *am*, what kind of Christian
Shylock would I be if I weren't beside

myself with bliss to help you, happy
as a Hukvaldy hound who's caught
the whiff of a fox: musty, magnificent?

When I wrote *The Cunning Little Vixen*,
I spent hours in the woods just listening
at the edge of a brackish pond. I wanted

to hear the frog's *brekete*, the mosquito's
*ssuiiih*: music that was not song. I wanted
the opera buff to feel mud oozing into his

polished black boots, or a trout dart under
her gown's velvet hem to skim her ankle.
I've been two days in this city, and already

I'm sick of all the smart people so bored
by crabapples and crows. Nature *is* cunning,
more than they'll ever know, surely cunning

enough, my vixen in the potato vines, to bring
*us* together, so bring your husband and son if
you must, but come to my cottage. The thought

of summer, the green glare of grass, unbroken
by your shadow crossing the field is unbearable.
The gold aria is nothing without its red throat.


Luhačovice, 21 August 1927

Darling darling darling,

I can't believe it was only yesterday
you were here. I took a mud bath
earlier, and the girl put a bog pack

on my back. I'm probably sprouting
pussywillows. What an idea: *taking
the waters.* Don't worry, from sulfur

baths to fizzing springs where I lie
tickled by a din of pins, I take, oh
I take. I'm not jealous of *David*,

but the air you breathe. I want to be
the blood blushing up your neck
as you read these words. Don't try

to deny it. I know you shut the door
of your sitting room before you slit
my letters with your nails. You can't

fool me. But of course you can: men
*are* fools. I watch their bellies buoyed
in our fake Roman baths as they play

chess under marble colonnades as if
their reign would last a millennium,
as if oblong jowls bobbing in steam

are a virgin's dream of virility. Do you
think I don't know I'm one of them?
Fleshy pashas whose marbled mass

has the mildew patina of temple ruins.
Aqueducts fracture. Love is forgotten
as quickly as the audience rushing for

a table at the bistro forgets the opera's
final note. The "glory" of art: we know
the color of the comb Nero ran through

his hair and know his chamber pot's
design, but who remembers the melody
he played as another atrium caught fire?

I know my fate, Kamila. Do you know
the source of the healing waters of our
majestic White Carpathians? Tourists,

invalids come from Berlin and Trieste
seeking cures—Lourdes with baccarat
and beer in place of the Virgin—but

under the soporific pools, the roulette
wheels, the picnics of salmon and cider
on banks so lush a lady can make love

without chafing her shoulder blades,
is a war that makes Verdun look like
a battle of red ants: magma churns just

under the crust, erupts in scoria, gouges
out trenches. We live on a cauldron's lid
in our calm gorge, and carnage in earth's

core carves the gorgeous high walls of our
Moravia, the crags we cherish, the waters
we take. Of course love shivered our lives.

What did we think it would do to them?

Luhačovice, 28 August 1927

You my soul of roses,

I go home tomorrow, discouraged as usual
I can't finish one fantasia. I can't concentrate
without you next to me any more than I can

with you here. But a strange thing happened
this morning as I sat by the carousel jotting
notes on the rhythms of footsteps: a cleric,

a shop girl, a dog chasing a cherry branch.
Suddenly there was a boy spilling cocoa
on my summer suit, and I began to weep.

His mother didn't know whether to slap me
to bring me to my senses or yell at her son,
who by now was fascinated, as if I were one

of those plaster statues of saints, tears welling
from its painted eyes, but he was determined
to examine me close enough to figure it out.

My Vladimír was stubborn like that when he
wanted to play with my watch, his small hands
working it out of its snug pocket. I think of him

every day, Kamila, but not with real feeling.
Then this morning I remembered everything,
but to call it *remembering* is laughable. When

I saw the suspenders on the toddler's overalls,
I was fastening little Vladíček's blue buttons
on Sunday morning. The wet, woolly smell

of the church and the taste of apple ice cream
we got on our way back home, even in winter,
mixed together in my mind, as they likely had

in his as well. How fast the brain must run
to keep pace with the heart! I saw pink ice
on his lips and then I was kissing the sweat

from his eyes when scarlet fever filled him
till there was no room for it and him in his
furnace of skin, and I was thinking of how

I would write this letter and of how grief
might win me more than an innocent kiss
the next time you walked down the yellow

sand path to my door, and thinking, too,
of scenes with the boy Aljeja in my *House
of the Dead*, how I must add a gay clarinet

and honking trombone to banish any whiff
of kitsch. The boy's mother was still gently
swabbing with her handkerchief the stains

from my lapel, and I thought—for the first
time!—what it must have meant to Zdenka
to come to me after our son's death, feral

with desire for another child, to ask me to take
the clips from her hair, and to watch me turn
and walk down the hall to our white piano.


Písek, 8 September 1927

My beloved, my one,

How can I sleep when you are two doors
down the hall, cuddled with your David
even if only listening to him snore? How

can *you* sleep? When I turn out the light
I imagine your bare feet pad down the hall
toward my room. David is a gracious host,

pouring cognac from his private decanter
to celebrate my quartet tonight. Can he know
what he was toasting? I must have been drunk

to attempt a trio based on Tolstoy's tale
of Beethoven's tour de force! Yes, it was
a trio, but something was missing. I can't

explain it, but when I tossed it into the fire,
our hound pawing the hearth to retrieve
the pages, as if they were a quail, without

singeing his old fur, I knew it had to be
a quartet. It's not that every marriage
is a triangle, though it is, but that every

triangle demands a quartet. I love it here
at your home, smoking your black cherry
blend among David's antiques, but I know

I must return to Zdenka. Without her,
my life is a melodrama instead of a novel,
nothing but *genre*, though I'd never admit it

to her. When you visit I pray your David
had never been born, but I know he's our
bedrock. That boring husband of yours

is our door to this world *and* the lustrous
underworld. Sparrows twitter as we stroll
through the dregs of your rose bower: so,

an adequate song, but David waxes
his moustache to prepare for a meeting
in Prague, and every gesture connects us

to the Hapsburg court, to interest rates
at London banks and to the fashion
for preparing Dover sole at the bankers'

private clubs, breaded cod at clerks' pubs.
I know I sound senile, but I'm singsong
if I'm cut off from the world, from crowns

and pfennigs and cents, from the centuries
of silver bonds and silk cravats. Tolstoy
was an ass, Kamila! You know he wrote

his *Kreutzer Sonata* to denounce music:
the sins it inspires in men, and in women.
Writers get old, but we musicians—never.

I wrote my quartet to defy him. I'll see
you and David for coffee at dawn, mud
on my boots but not a crease in my suit,

a tulip's crimson grace note in my lapel.


Brno, 1 January 1928

Kamila!

Yes, my third letter to you today. You decide
which to burn. I know you sometimes snip,
without a flinch, a line or two. I'm wearing

the red tie you gave me for St. Wenceslas;
it's stuck in my heart with Zdenka's diamond
stud. She went to bed hoarse from shouting.

I'd told her I wanted to visit you on my way
to Prague. "Eighty kilometers," she shrieked,
"eighty kilometers out of your way!" slamming

the door to her room but making sure I could
hear her sobbing. The day she is silent: that's
the day I fear. I'm 73, and I know less now

than the day I was born. I think my mother
loved me and I loved her, but Zdenka . . .
is it love, pride, *forte, piano*? She broke

the lock on my one treasure, the hand-carved,
hand-painted chest with its blurred, blemished
gold fleur-de-lys—searching for your letters.

When all she found were my manuscripts,
how could she have known in their stuttering
ostinatos, their augmented fifths and falling

thirds, even the sleigh bells I put in the score
of my *Katya*, they held more of my dark soul
than a cupboard of letters. I opened my desk

and hurled the whole batch at her, daring her
to find one word that would hint at our guilt.
I knew there was none: in ten years you've not

once opened your heart. You've been cold
as the aquavit those Finns drink straight
on thin ice while they watch their pulsing,

fluttering northern lights. Do you know that
some people claim to have *heard* the aurora?
They say it makes a soft snapping, like a fawn

following its mother through the forest. What
I'd give to hear that! Some say it doesn't exist,
but I know. You've given me that, my fickle,

wet-winged red vanessa. How could Zdenka
think I would ever give you up? You must
forgive what I said before, though I won't

blot it out. Let it stand, with the rest of my
crackling static. It's almost morning. I touch
my crystal flute in Brno to yours in my heaven.

Prague, 8 April 1928, after the derby

My only Kamilka,

My blood is hot enough to boil spaetzle
for the venison we should roast to feast
and mark this happiest day of my life:

*you* are my wife, I swear to the Virgin.
Each time our horse cleared a hurdle
or stream in the steeplechase, I knew

I was right about you: you'd do anything
for love, anything to win, fanning flushed
cheeks with a smudged program under

your hat's green satin brim, the same one
you wore on Friday to Karlštejn Castle.
It matched the garnet-encrusted walls

of the oratory where Karel IV prayed
in the 14th Century, a servant sliding
open an iron grate to leave him food

as if he were a prisoner. The tower's view
of vineyards and silver spruce in the valley
below is something I still can't talk about,

and I don't know how you eluded David.
Maybe you put a wishbone's jinx on him,
my gypsy witch. When you held my hand

to your neck so I could feel the pulse, I saw
we were alone in one of the castle gardens,
all blinding plum trees and Easter lilies,

as close as we've ever been, and as far. I think
when you love someone, you love their skin
more than anything. Zdenka's has always

been fair as ewe's milk—we'd joke about
where our Olga got her dark hazel—it's
strange, you don't look like Olga at all but—

this is the first I've noticed: you have her skin.
I must have sensed it the first time I saw you.
*You have her skin.* It's been twenty-five years,

but doesn't even feel like yesterday: it's *today*
she's wracked with the typhus and I'm still
at her bedside, taking notes as my daughter

dictates the instructions for her own funeral.
She begged me to finish *Jenufa* so she could
hear it before she died. I couldn't do it, but

I took down the rhythm and pitch of every
cough and slurred syllable: I used them all.
I can't recall her voice anymore, but its timbre

fills each measure I write. I didn't want her
when she was born. Now sometimes I wake
at night and can't remember how to breathe,

and the instant before I do is the only time
I feel truly myself. Zdenka and I are under
a curse, and it's too late to rescind: hammers

on the drums' taut skins can't be unstruck.
Does it matter whom we kiss in gaudy masks
twining the maypole on Midsummer Eve?

If through you I can love my child, or a god
I don't believe in but for his malice, or even
my wife, who walked shyly into my studio

fifty years ago and played Chopin like rain
falling at night on a hotspring, unaware
I'd destroy her life, how can I refuse?

Tomorrow I go home to the orchards
of my Moravia and their almost ecstatic
despair. I'll write more, my dearest, my

hive of choirs, the very minute I arrive.

# TUNING PEGS

## GALILEO'S NOTES

Galileo worked at night, able to see light-years
farther in the dark. We're nocturnal beasts.
My father taught me to study the sun during
an eclipse, spicules rising. One Ukiah night
Virginia and I sat in the back of her pickup,
the silence awkward and natural, like sex
the first time, brains chock with sensation
(as if entering a hotel room in a strange city,
Miraflores or Miami) and bodies wanting
nothing but to be. To see a person just *being*,
an animal drinking at a river, taking its time,
is almost obscene. Galileo was not a believer,
but like my father at night at our kitchen table,
his glass of milk as luminous and conservative
as a candle, he took his precise, furious notes,
seeing Jupiter's four moons for the first time—
icy Europa, white and smooth as mozzarella,
and Io's red, volcanic stew—through lenses
ground with his own hands. We love most
the places inside us even God has not seen.

# AURORA

*In 1613 Jakob Boehme published* Aurora, *outlining the seven stages of the spiritual path.*

## I. THE ABYSS (BOEHME AT HIS BENCH, 1623, GOERLITZ)

For a cobbler to write of the Abyss
and the light it devoured—Blasphemy!
Pastor Richter bellowed from his pulpit,
but he underestimated my faith's iron.
I'd already been told it was a sin
to aspire even to the butcher's daughter,
but Catharina and I had four sons!
Four sons and three daughters and still
I strapped the leather to the last at dawn
and honed my holy pentateuch of knives.
For five years I kept silent, pen on parchment
usurped by awl on leather. The bitterness
of God: I know it in all the bones of my hand.

Faith? I believe only what my hands hold,
eyes behold, but *nota bene* once is enough
for me to know what I know. I told Catharina
I loved her once, on our wedding night,
when she held my thumb to her pulse
as if to the kick of an imp in her womb,
and the words leapt out of me like oil
from a skillet, like God's exclamation
when he felt our first gasp, the tug within
Him as we sucked our very air out of His
vast lungs: didn't he reveal everything then
we needed to hear? Isn't that our original
sin—to extort from God a confession
of His love for us? I can't bear
you looking at me, Catharina,
my Catya, I've hardly been a father
or a man. The thought of your forgiveness
appalls me . . .

## II. Salt (Catharina's retort)

It's not as if I ever thought, Jakob,
you and Father would get along,
you with your blades sheer as fish scales,
him with his cleaver. Don't you know yet
how much we're alike—your ability
to peel the seven skins of the divine,
and mine to distinguish the ox's
blood from its bone marrow,
the angelic pink blood of the pig
from the black river sluicing through
the exposed shoulder blades of the steer,
and the calf's pale, cloying ichor? I know
all these and more. I'm your match. I'm
your wife. I'm your brine. Twelve years
from your vision until your *Aurora*,
and I was your vessel, listening to you
as I boiled the leeks and brisket and
even that was Father's gift. You sunk
your sulfurous songs in my saltwater,
and I kept them fresh, secure, where no
cruel tongue could touch them
but yours, until they were cured
all the way to the fat in the bone.

## III. Sulfur (Pastor Richter at the pulpit)

*Behold, I send you forth as sheep*
*in the midst of wolves.* Thus says
Our Lord: wolves are among us.
What are the signs by which a wolf
can be recognized? One who lives
on the edge but lives off the center,
the fat of the lamb. The wolf is proud
of his independence, of his solitude.
I rose this morning to pray: I saw
an ordinary girl—you all know her—
up long before me, spatters of milk

already dappling her lap from work
in her dark barn. I saw a man,
weary from heaving bales, haul
hides on his back to the tannery—
he's with us now, aching but hungry
for the Word of God. I saw a woman,
her spine curved from churning butter,
in pain on our hardwood but happy
to be here. All these, all these the wolf
considers beneath him. He may smile
when you pass in the street or transact
business, but do not be fooled: he feels
only contempt. I understand contempt
for a shepherd like me. I confess I am
comfortable. This morning I had plum
jam and biscuits after prayer. I accept
the wolf's contempt. I welcome it.
But contempt for His sheep: this,
brothers and sisters, Our Lord
does not forgive. The wolf lives
off the succulent flesh of the lamb
even as he sneers at its innocence,
but no matter what he consumes,
his own flesh does not moisten,
nor is it palatable. Our Lord spits
gristle from His hallowed mouth.

What are the signs? The Word is clear:
*If I have the gift of prophecy and know all*
*mysteries and have not charity, I am nothing.*
The wolf is among us, one who knows
the seven levels of angels and who can
discriminate seraphim from dominions,
but does not love. We don't have to ask
what must be done. Our Lord tells us:
*Be harmless as doves.* And so we shall.
Let it be known that we wish no harm
to any soul who inhabits the soft banks
of the Oder in Goerlitz. Let it be known

we are pleased to be harmless as doves
and wise as serpents. Let us praise the wolf
as he steps, warily, among jagged stones,
cloistral crevices, day after day after day.


## IV. MERCURY (JAKOB'S CONFESSION)

Words! In the year of Our Lord 1600
I *saw* a plank of light strike a pewter bowl
as soft as rabbit's piss falls in the rain
on a bed of thyme, and for twenty years
I've been grasping at words to explain.
A worm's way to truth, nothing but false
turns, churning light and loam into shit—
that's all that words have been to me,
and they've been my life. Don't talk
to me about the Word. If you must,
talk about stitches: the tunnel, the raw
linen thread that flows from the grain
into a bootsole's flesh without emerging;
the whip, used by the few who know it
to bind the lining invisibly to the interior;
the flesh-edge, entering the leather's pulp
and exiting not the other side but the rim;
and the one I love most, the shoemaker's
stitch itself, the saddle—two needles,
one on each end of the thread, passing
each other in the quick dark. Tell me
of the stitch of the curved awl, the stab
of the straight, and when each is used.
Tell me what I saw. I know better
than any how much I've presumed.
A pewter dish. A few minutes later
and Catharina would have filled it
with soup and I would not have seen,
and yet that to-be-filled *is* what I saw.
I saw its to-be-filled by Catya's hooked
tin ladle. Then I saw all at once its to-be-
dented, its to-have-been-beaten,-cast-and-

buffed, its to-have-been-born in Cornish
tin mines by tired men slogging through
undrained shafts, its to-have-been-spun
on lathes and imbued with a gray sheen
from lead that might have lined a noble's
coffin, its soon-to-hold broth for my brats,
and its to-be-melted-down in time and reborn
as candlestick, chamberpot, tankard, chalice.
What I saw was a pewter bowl pure as the light
that clashed it like a cymbal, but what I saw too
was light that was pocked, toxic, a palimpsest
layered and patinaed, yet plain as a soup bowl.

### V. WATER (JAKOB'S SON CONFIDES IN HIS MOTHER)

Do you ever think it was a curse
to give me his name? Jakob: saved
by his mother's love when his father
spurned him. *And Isaac loved Esau,*
*but Rebekah loved Jakob.* The Bible
also says: *he refused to be comforted.*
I was so scared, Mother, when he died
I hid behind the pine tree and watched
the worshippers deface his grave, as if
everything he'd turned his face from
all his life, all he'd left for *us* to see to—
egg yolk, pig blood, coal tar (we nursed
each black chip so he could be warm)—
had returned to exact vengeance, paint
itself on his stone as the defaced mask
by which he'd be known in eternity:
defined by the good folk of Goerlitz.
I'm not ashamed I didn't face them,
but that I lacked courage to join in.
I hid there and I thrilled as the sexton
took his hammer to the cross and left it
a stump. With all his white mercury
Father couldn't transform himself,
though gold etched the Oder River

that morning he rowed away on his barge
of hobnail boots he dreamed would save us
when he sold them to soldiers on the front.
Pathetic man! Plague and an empty purse
are all that brought him home. In Jesus'
name I forgive those who hurt me, but
Jesus did not live to see what was done
to His mother. There's nothing for you
to say. I'm leaving you with the geese.
The river is tolerant. Through freshets
and eddies, chop and trough, riff and
gurge, from backwater to Stettin Bay,
it carries skins, metals, blood and ale,
bakers, whores, Catholics and slick-
whiskered rats on its back. I believe
it will carry me. *I believe*: the two words
Father never wanted spoken in his house.


## VI. Resonance (Catharina replies)

You missed the sunrise the morning
you were born, but I'll never forget:
each layer of cloud a different hue,
claret to ale, like the white towels
and sheets on my bed, some soaked,
some barely damp, with afterbirth
and waters. The crowning sun.
For once, everything was body,
so clear and peaceful. And then you
began to suck—so hard the universe
had to give up exactly what you wanted,
no more; just as it had, my love, for me.

Your father loved you with such a fury,
Jakob, as a deaf man loves music, the four
voices of the organ's fugue he senses only
through the church floor's wooden shudder.

## VII. MYSTERY (BOEHME DIES OF A FEVER, 1624)

I hear music, Catya, but it must be
other angels, not the ones I dreamed of.
I had to leave: I was useless, though you
won't be surprised I was of no more use
on a battlefield, with my cart of thread
and leather. *You* could have conjured
a broth out of roast greens and roots!
I got so sick the wounded gave me
their whiskey; the healthy cursed me.
Yes, I laughed too: it was so familiar,
but the prayers I learned were new: awe
of a man at dusk watching a rabbit cower
in sparse grass, the miracle of its scrawn
feeding a regiment; and the soft orison
of powder tamped down a musket's bore.
I don't blame them for mocking me
as a prophet, but I tell you: the killing
will not cease for a thousand years,
because the only testimony of the dead
is dumb blood. The prayers that survive
are the prayers of the survivors, who swear
(*we* swear) never again, but the obscene
thrill was thrust in their veins with rusted
blades, and they will come back for more.

We'd gotten as far as the White Mountains
outside Prague when Ferdinand crushed us.
I'd looked forward to Tycho Brahe's tomb
in the Tyn Cathedral. Wouldn't you know
I'd be a tourist even in war? But think of it:
the first astronomer to look so intensely
at the heavens he saw the birth of a star,
a virgin birth the Papists couldn't allow,
for it proved (the scandal!) things change.
Now he lies in a tomb under the weight
of a pair of spires. Such a fuss over a star.
Sometimes I lie in bed in the morning
coughing as rain falls from the eaves

transmuting nothing. Don't be afraid.
If they ruin my grave it's only to rage
at their own. I know better than any
how righteous is their wrath. Who was I
to scorn the Madonna's icon when I had
nothing to replace it but a joke, a zodiac
clock tower with numbers in gold code?
No one can make sense of my scribbling,
least of all those who love me. The axes'
ringing is my best requiem. God's clerks
will hear it. Only falling water might speak
for me better. For years I sought the music
of the spheres, but now I realize: angels
don't make music, Catya. They dance
to the music *we* make, of jawbone, gut
and hair—they dance in my black shoes.

## THE ORIGIN OF POETRY

Not the astronomer but the accountant
slicing olives for his egg salad sandwich
before resuming his ledger. The first writing
was the kingdom's accounts: 22,000 sheaves
in the granary, 600 head of spotted cattle,
a queen's 12 gold combs. The first poem:
whoever wrote it must have suspected
he had the *goods* on the Pharaoh: words
more real than things. The salsal bird
cracks one barley seed with its beak
on the greenest branch of the tamarisk.
A barge with reed baskets full of lettuce
and casks of resin is dragged downriver
by slaves on the bank grasping taut ropes.
The scribe takes it all down with his stylus
and one day notices the jagged gold stripe
on the gills of the azagur, who are owned
by no one, and thinks to write *it* down,
along with the number of sila of wheat
on the 480 iku of fields he has surveyed.
Soon, that word is written whose exact
meaning is unknown but is translated
as *that without which life is not possible,*
and the hawsers' creak notches higher.

## STILL LIFE WITH PEARS

— *Translated from the Frisian*

Leeuwarden, 7 April 1891

Dear Arjen,

I don't know why I want to write you
now. I can't believe it's been five years
you dragged your trunk down an icy pier
to board a steamer bound for New York
just to be hauled by train to that place
that sounds so alien, *Iowa*, searching for—
what was it?—richer earth, big potatoes.
Aunt Annika says that you've found it,
but (God forgive me) I have to laugh:
a place where cows are fed—what is it?—
*corn*. The milk must taste so strange!
This morning in one of the creameries
in the old part of town I found a cheese
that had the aroma of potter's clay
and tasted like caramel. I've lived here
since I was a girl and never known this!
Please forgive the blotches, but my pen
has a mind of its own, and in any case,
I half suspect by the time you get this
you will have forgotten our language.

Today was the first the daylight loitered
late enough I could walk along the canal,
the reflections the dark cherry and maple
of the minister's furniture. You remember
Jarig, don't you? He hasn't changed: always
kind, the way a granite sea wall is kind.

I hesitate to tell you, but I have a friend
who buys me the baubles I let him know
I want. He's a butter merchant; his ramekins
sell as delicacies as far away as London.
Do you remember our green front doors,
each with its identical mail slot of brass?

Sometimes I think to hear from you, but
the truth is I look more for the weeklies.
The truth is I'm pleased to live in a place
where the brick façade of every edifice
shows a chalk line where the water rose
when the dikes were overwhelmed.
It's not danger I crave, just knowledge,
like the knowledge of the shadows cast
by a bowl of pears, and I know you had
at least that to take with you to your new
habitat that Annika says is a floodplain,
like the fields that edge our River Linde.

I'm sure what I've told you means nothing,
and what you're curious to hear I've forgotten
to say, but I want to get back now to my soup
and my novel. You remember my soup of cider
and white beans! But I won't get sentimental—
it's the novel you'd like: a French grenadier
shot filching eggs from a farm outside Lyon.

Don't you see? You made the wrong
decision: it's irrevocable. *I'm the one
who's free.* Who would have guessed?
The lamps come on along the canal.
Now when I button my coat I can feel
brass scratch on gabardine. Evening
the shade of Spanish figs. I can hear
my heels echo on stones rinsed clean
by merchants closing for the night,
all down the alley past the library,
the wine shop, the mildew-spotted
gate I found that hides a guelder rose.
I say goodbye for now. Always, your

Tetja

## CONCERTO IN E MINOR

> *"Who am I when I'm not playing the cello?"*
> —Jacqueline du Pré

### ADAGIO – MODERATO

Don't you dare answer that rabid phone
when your most ravishing patient is here
to see you, Doctor. It's a C sharp, Amadeo,

that ring! I've still got perfect pitch, even if
some days my vibrato is harsh as that racket.
It hurts my ears, Doctor Limentani: it hurts,

Lemon Drops, like the Ukrainian folk songs
Dad played on his accordion, a dull stab
as if I were late again on one of my tours

and the pilot were making his descent
to Heathrow or Tel Aviv or Chicago
too fast: someone twists the tuning

pegs a half turn tighter in my head.
But I can't fool you, can I? You know
I love the descent. That long, melodic

line in the Brahms that comes down
like a queen in ten kilos of blue silk
who without a glance goes out the arch

past the formal gardens to her fishpond,
trailing her muddy raiment. That's how
it felt when Daniel kissed me, after I taught

him how. But he was always a quick study,
not like my students, dense as Dover biscuits
with ginger jam: they've got as much music

in them as my sister Hil's chickens—cluck,
twitch, scratch and then that horrid muffled
*plouf* as the egg is expelled, their bland opus.

I tell you, Amadeo, even my cleverest girls
confuse passion with speed. Danny
never made that mistake. I tell them

not just to play a note *adagio* or even
*largo*, but to play it *forever*. That's what
it was like when he first touched me:

clavicle, scapula, ilium (that's my ass,
Lemon Drops, just in case you failed
anatomy), and that puffy place in back

of my knee, the fossa (I've become quite
good at crosswords now that I can't even
manage a bow—I can't even fork a shrimp

on crushed ice), that place soft as a mollusk
and just as delectable, as Danny discovered.
He knew how to do *forever*. I'd always been

a pale hunk of dough, and I was rising
that day at 102°, laid flat on my bed as if
it were Mum's breadboard, legs clutching

the cello like a rolling pin (I'd spew if
I sat up to play), the glands in my neck
and groin swollen like pasty dumplings.

I was a sight for Danny's own red eyes:
he had the fever, too, and when his hands
claimed as his own (never again Brahms')

those twelve-note chords, my arm sawed
the bow as no blonde bird ever had before,
cut through the music's thick bark, through

the juicy sapwood, down to the heartwood,
the pith. Yes, you could say we were in love.
I loved all of him, seven octaves and more,

from the calfskin of his Italian wing-tips
and the snipped caps of his Havana cigars
to his zeal for the orange groves of Zion.

It began as a lark: I'd be a Jew for Daniel.
I would have been a Zoroastrian for him,
God knows, or even an Irish Catholic.

Mum brought the plum tart to the table
on Christmas Eve, and Hilary and I laughed
at the baby Jesus till the brandied hard sauce

shot up our noses: that's what conversion was,
at first. Hil and I had a bomb patch behind
the Wendy house Dad built for us, a field

where we'd hide under the clematis vines.
We called it that because we half-remembered
Mum's stories of her and Dad honeymooning

in a shelter during the blitz: they were happy
with their wireless and tins of smoked meat,
for once. One thing I'd prayed for was not to

end up like them, so of course I found myself
looking for a wedding dress in Jerusalem
during the Six Day War, playing for soldiers

from the back of a lorry. What I'd found
in the bomb patch under green apples and
found later in the cello—it has a woman's

voice, you know, not mine, a clove-skinned
girl chanting in a foreign tongue as she rises,
dripping, from the mikvah—and what I

found in my new religion were the same:
music that gave me the chutzpah to say
what no one would hear but was obvious

even on my wedding day with its stars big
as begonias, night jasmine kicking the door ajar,
and is clear to anyone who rides the tube

from Brixton to Barnet: *no messiah has come.*
The hour's up and your next patient's here
in the waiting room, and once again, Amadeo,

we haven't fucked. Did I tell you how I pass
the time between visits? Translating *fuck*
into every language. I'll bring you the list:

it's a scroll, a torah. See you Tuesday, luv.


### LENTO – ALLEGRO MOLTO

Look at me, Amadeo, I'm such a *klots.*
I kicked one of the cobbles by your gate
and went down like a camel on the Sinai.

Look at my bloody knee. Stones! Pebble,
boulder: they're all a curse to me. Damn
Dad and his whole polished collection.

We'd spend summers on Jersey, us kids
and Mum stringing jewelry on the sand
out of cowries and winkles, while Dad

slogged off with his ridiculous goggles
and beloved hammer to hunt his rocks—
he wanted basics, no beauties for him,

no garnet or jasper, just granite, gneiss,
and the stuff so old it didn't even breach
the earth's surface when a volcano burst,

just cooled, bided its time underground,
and grew pink crystals. One feldspar vein
was all the beauty Dad could stand.

I see you thinking, Amadeo, thinking
how much I'm like him. Aren't you
clever? He couldn't wait to get home

to his tumbler in the cellar; he'd polish
the stones for a month, the unceasing
noise like a ship's hull lurching inch

by gritty inch beneath our snug beds.
We heard it in our dreams. Last night
I dreamed of a hat and a silly sarong

that looked like something I'd spend
too much on at Harrods—all splayed
on a beach—and I stepped gingerly

because I knew there was someone there,
listening to the *wish* of heels in sand, but
there was no body. *There was no body.*

What if Dad outlives me? The thought
of him wheezing, a punctured bagpipe,
at my grave, bravely stifling his nausea

at the Star of David to lay a round stone
on my tomb to trumpet his respect—
one of those same shitty gobs of schist

he'd chip off Jersey cliffs: I can see him
in his glasses at my grave, wandering off
(just like a Jew!) looking for specimens.

Promise me you won't let it happen
that way. Our wedding was priceless:
we gave Mum and Dad 48 hours' notice

to get their Christian asses to Jerusalem,
and they did. Mum perched on her heels
with the women for hours, while the men

sat in the center of the courtyard—Christ,
it was hot! Sweating like a trussed pig
in my layers of gauze, I felt as out of place

as roast pork—*I am the rose of Sharon,*
the cantor sang from the Song of Songs—
Hilary had to laugh when a rooster paraded

in the dust, and the goat-reek overwhelmed
the bouquets—*thy love is better than wine*—
I felt woozy beneath the billowing chuppah—

*cluster of camphire in the vineyards*—swaddled
in veils as the rabbi read the seven blessings—
*the clefts of the rock, secret places of the stairs,*

Daniel ground the wineglass into the stone
with his heel—*a hart among the mountains
of spices*—and they gave me my new name,

Shulamite—*and he feedeth among the lilies.*
It was sweet, Lemon Drops, but the peace
about as brief as the cease-fire when Syria

withdrew from the Golan Heights.
Danny and I got drunk. The tanks
had gone as far as the Suez Canal

and the Gulf of Aqaba, taken back
the Old City, and we paid no attention
to the occasional grenade on the street,

like the tingling I ignored in my fingers.
Who thought I'd lose anything so plain
as the feel of bow hair on the D string,

a skill as routine as chopping parsley?
Isn't it amazing, Amadeo, the care I'd
give an instrument? I'd yell at bellhops

to raise the temperature three degrees,
to fix the *humidity*, as if they could don
a bonnet and make rain, and all because

I was afraid for the varnish, for a strain
at the belly seam, and who knows what
the fog might do to my bloody F-holes.

Maybe I wouldn't be sick if *I'd* been shipped
from gig to gig in a silver-velvet-lined case.
They say a genius can think two thoughts

at once, like the talons of my left hand
sinking into a note while my right arm
caresses it with the bow. That's why MS

is the genius disease: it makes you pee
in your pantyhose, blurs your vision and
caves in your knees all at the same time.

I've had boyfriends who couldn't do *that*.
Multiple sclerosis: its dirty teeth strip
the insulation off your nerves, and mine

were already pretty raw. Shalom, ducks.


**ADAGIO**

I'm wrecked, Amadeo. This morning Hilary
came to visit me in the jaws, so to speak. So
to speak. Hilfire and brimstone gone over

the brim: she'd do anything for me. I had her
cut my hair. How's it look? My sweet Hilcat,
my big sister: she'd snatch me from *His* jaws

to carry me in hers and lay me in lavender.
She went to Asia just to bring me home
for brekkers, bangers and tea on the farm,

just to dance. I was dying to ditch Danny,
and so we celebrated the High Hilly Days
at Ashmansworth. I was so happy to be home

with my Hilly Ghost, her little fire tongue
playing lickety-lick with the lemon curd
on Christmas morn, my Hilly and her ivy—

*and the holly bears a berry as red as any blood.*
How could I have done it, Amadeo, to *her*,
my Hilley's Comet? I didn't even want him.

Their stone farmhouse got so cold at night
they let me have the attic, and even there
I had to tuck up my knees in my thick

Guernsey jumper to sleep. I'd hear him
in the mornings chopping wood while Hil
was gossiping with the Rock Cornish hens.

She still thinks I envied her ordinary life—
so down-to-earth and predictable (the return
to the tonic at the end of a sonata), her cheese-

fermenting, husband-humping rites of spring,
but she's the most extraordinary person I've
ever known. I never gave a fig for her farm

or her farmer, though Kif *was* cute, wiping off
his Wellingtons before he'd cross the threshold
and sit down for his mince pie. I'd be shivering

by the time I heard his wool socks on the stairs.
Hil had slowed her breath like Mum taught her
to toughen her lungs for the flute, and convinced

Kiffer she was asleep, but I knew she could hear
every lunge and giggle—God, I did it *for* her.
When I got warm enough to tug off my mittens

and toss them to kingdom come, she could hear—
when I struck a match and lit the petrol lamp
to see what we were doing, she could hear—

when we talked and talked—not after, *during*—
and compared the shapes we saw in the shadows
that lightning made on the bureau (a salmon, no

a postbox)—and she could hear it when at last
I fell asleep: a sound like gannets' wings when
they stop beating and glide toward oyster beds.

Hilary knew me better than you do, Lem:
she knew me to my entrails. When I played
the Saint-Saëns, I *was* the swan: imperial,

arrogant, serene, snow melting on a lake.
We'd learned from Dad's rock hunts:
he attacked the stone with his chisel,

broke it open to the jagged green glass,
and music was violence in our family,
even as we set the tea cakes on the doily.

The attack of bow on string, swanlike
legato, flying staccato, was relentless,
and Hilary still knows how to wield

the clef and stave better than anyone I know.
I wanted *her*, Amadeo. That's what it must
have been, and Kiffer was just the *medium*,

like the radio on the sideboard, sturdy but
crackling with static, when we kids listened
to Mum's recitals. When I kissed his wide

open eyes, how could I not have seen it?
It was her I was holding with all my famous
lissome limbs (I'd have hung from the man

if I'd had a tail)—it was always her I wanted:
our talks at midnight about the hurdy-gurdy
grinder at Hyde Park—God, I miss her! Shit,

I bit my lip and it's bleeding, Lem. Every time
I shagged him and sang *God Save the Queen* or
made him listen to my Schumann recording

for the Schumpteenth time, it was her. Music's
not much to live on, you know. The repertoire
may be a thousand hours but it all comes down

to that one chord in the third movement or
the moment when the rhythm shifts gears
in the scherzo and roars—it's so easy to hear

everything but what matters, but she gets it.
I held her hard husband as hard as the snow
holds a field of clover, as the cello holds its note,

its creamy secret, in its spruce box even as it fills
the Royal Hall. She's the only one who forgave me
not out of love but out of something else, almost

mathematical, like music: the piece demanded it.


### ALLEGRO – MODERATO – ADAGIO, MA NON TROPPO

Where were we last time, Lemon Drops?
I seem to recall a naked flautist; maybe
it was a dream. This morning Ruth Ann

gave me my sponge bath: believe me,
that's *not* who I want to remind me of
my body. I'd rather you undertook

that chore, Amadeo. As a rule I feel
like a shucked brain in a wheelchair,
about as appetizing as a soft-boiled egg,

or the squid Danny and I ate at the Ritz,
marinated in their own ink. I'm a mess,
a bombed-out outhouse, an earth closet,

but I'm getting used to it. Not that I'm
hopeless: I managed to hit the cow's-eye
when I flung my pea soup in Ruth Ann's

ruddy face when she started her harangue
on how there'd be a miracle if I'd come
back to Jesus and his red heart that looks

like organ meat. Don't you love giblets?
Sometimes she puts my bow in my hand
in case Jesus has stormed my barricades—

Christ, I can't even open the damn case.
I'd already played the Elgar Concerto
when I first saw the old man's photo.

He looked like Dad to me! It was awful:
I could see him driving our green Wolseley
slowly down the ruts into town for oatcakes

and tea, but I got over it. The Elgar's *mine*.
I'd pluck one string and it could be heard
over the whole brass. Bring on the winds

and percussion: I'd whisper and an audience
would hear every note as if I were alone,
and in a way I was. I'd play as if brushing

my hair (always too fine to be held back
by a clip), then as if I were water falling
(I had a special endpin built so the cello

would stand straighter and gravity take
possession of my cascading arm), and
sometimes as if I were that American

prizefighter, Cassius Clay, who hits
so fast you can't see it and proclaims
the round his opponent will go down—

I did concerts like that, sweat drenching
my knickers while I made it look easy.
When I'm not playing the cello, Amadeo,

who am I? Don't lie. It's my instrument,
my *tool*. *Homo habilis*, Doc: the definition
of man is handyman. Without our tools

we're animals, crustaceans or anemones,
and that's just how I feel, a rubbery tube,
one end an open mouth and the other

sucking on stone. They're called flowers
of the sea with their mauve and orange
tentacles: cold comfort that is. Hil and I

found them in tidepools all summer long
at St. Catherine's Breakwater: anemones,
whelks, limpets, fantastic peacock worms.

Once we even found a sunstar, round
as our kitchen clock. We thought of it
moving with imperceptible scrunches

across the sand in the shallow water
as we ran screaming back to the house
before the tide rose. That's what I love

about the Elgar: it turns its back even
on the sunset, defies that exotic beauty,
odalisque in red culottes and gold cuffs,

as soon as it parts the boudoir curtain,
and goes back to its peat bog cottage,
stokes the coals alone. It's merciless.

It reminds me of you when time's up,
but I know you miss me. Even with my ass
fattened up from the steroids, I know

I'm the sexiest item on your long agenda.
Your smile is professional, but I'm right.
You're too smart to lie to me about *that*.

As I tell my students, Amadeo, make sure
the string is vibrating *before* you touch it
with the bow. They must have tuned *me* up

before I was born: my high-frequency hum
always on edge, and peace is hell. The one
good thing about this disease is it always

comes up with a surprise, a fat firecracker
whose fuse is your nerves, when you think
it can't get worse. I'm almost blind now.

Here's a hoot: the Duke wanted to name
a rose after me so they gave me a choice,
but I couldn't see the blooms—or I could

see them but they all looked alike, bloody
onions on skewers—I wanted to pop them
on a grill, not hold them in my chafed arms

like a scullery maid. Finally I shut my eyes
so I could cast my vote by the scent alone.
One reminded me of the desert, something

in the air on my wedding night when I got
out of bed and looked out the open window.
I don't even think it was roses. I chose that one,

and told the Duke to call the thing the Wailing
Wall, not Jacqueline du Pré. At Ashmansworth
there were miles and miles of fuchsia hedges . . .

Did I ever tell you, Doctor Limentani, when
I decided to be a cellist? It was in Leningrad.
I'd been up all night playing Shostakovich

and Bach and Prokofiev—you know I never
practice: I *perform* even when I play alone
in a hotel room with my underwear soaking

in a basin I had to bribe a maid to bring me—
and that's after I've had enough vodka for a fat
Russian swan to swim in. God, those people

are tough, Lemon Drops! During the 900
days of the siege of Leningrad not one elm
or linden in the Summer Garden was cut

for fire by a freezing people: they wouldn't
sacrifice their stately avenues. Three A.M.
and already sunrise: that's what they mean

by the white nights of the Neva. I walked
along the embankment, saw the reflections
of the bridge and its lattice of wrought iron,

and I *knew*. Never, Amadeo, there is never
a moment when I'm not playing the cello.
White nights! I've had more than my share.

The manager had to pound on my door
and ask me to decrescendo my sforzandos.
I was still playing it—the final movement

of the Elgar—with the force of the ocean
bashing itself on the Jersey cliffs. You know
how the poor apparatchik felt, don't you?

Trying to shut me up. The light is strong
at 3 A.M. It made a deafening noise falling
on the quiet river. No one had to give me

a fucking Strad. I would have hammered
a spoon on iron pans till the dented silver
rippled like that river, just to be part of it.

Here comes that bore up the stairs again,
Amadeo, to take my place on your pouffy
Turkish couch. Let's make her wait, just

today. What a bird-watcher. What a bitch.